W9-BCX-938

DATE DUE

Shapes around Town

Circles
around Town

by Nathan Olson

Capstone
press

Mankato, Minnesota

A+ Books are published by Capstone Press,
151 Good Counsel Drive, P.O. Box 669, Mankato, Minnesota 56002.
www.capstonepress.com

1 2 3 4 5 6 11 10 09 08 07 06

Library of Congress Cataloging-in-Publication Data
Olson, Nathan.
    Circles around town / by Nathan Olson.
    p. cm.—(A+ books. Shapes around town)
    Summary: "Simple text, photographs, and illustrations help readers identify circles that can be found in a
city"—Provided by publisher.
    Includes bibliographical references and index.
    ISBN-13: 978-0-7368-6368-1 (hardcover)
    ISBN-10: 0-7368-6368-0 (hardcover)
    1. Circle—Juvenile literature. 2. Shapes—Juvenile literature. I. Title. II. Series.
QA484.O47 2007
516'.152—dc22   2005034808

Credits
Jenny Marks, editor; Kia Adams, designer; Renée Doyle, illustrator; Kelly Garvin,
    photo researcher/photo editor

Photo Credits
Capstone Press/Kay Olson, 4, 5
Corbis/Alan Schein Photography, 16; Bob Krist, 12; David Ball, 21; Douglas Mesney, 24–25;
    Guang Niu/Reuters, 9; J L de Zorzi, 17; John Brecher, 22–23; John McAnulty, 6;
    Kevin R Morris, 20; L. Nelson/Stock Photos/zefa, 8; Natalie Fobes, 19; Richard Cummins, 7, 13
Getty Images Inc./The Image Bank/Alan Becker, 10; The Image Bank/Ghislain & Marie David
    de Lossy, 11; Photodisc Blue Collection, cover; Stone/Reza Estakhrian, 18
Image Farm, 26, 27
Shutterstock/Tonis Valing, 14–15

Note to Parents, Teachers, and Librarians
The Shapes around Town set uses color photographs and a nonfiction format to introduce readers
to the shapes around them. *Circles around Town* is designed to be read aloud to a pre-reader, or to be
read independently by an early reader. Images and activities help early readers and listeners perceive
and recognize shapes. The book encourages further learning by including the following sections: Table
of Contents, Which Are Circles?, Welcome to Circle Town, Glossary, Read More, Internet Sites, and
Index. Early readers may need assistance using these features.

Table of Contents

What Is a Circle?

Circles are flat, round shapes with no straight sides. Let's look for circles all around town.

This perfectly round circle lets
light inside a city building.

Not all curved shapes are circles.
This big open shape is an oval.
It is not perfectly round.

This sharp circle quickly cuts through wood.

These big circles are giant pipes.
Look closely. How many circles
do you see?

Circles for Sale

Circles fill the bakery windows. How many tasty circles can you count?

10

These baskets are round, and so
are the peaches inside them. How
many circles do you see?

Look at all the shapes on this store's wall. Which are circles?

13

The sign at the zoo has
two large circles.

Some signs in the city glow bright.
Can you find two small circles
inside the big circle?

Circles with a slash tell people something is not allowed. What do these circles say is not allowed in the city park?

Traffic lights are circles stacked on top of each other. The green circle means GO.

This circle at the ballpark
shows off the city's team.

Fun Circles

Some circles make a big booming noise.

This tall circle lifts you high in the air.

Circles at the playground are lots of fun. Grab a circle and hang on tight!

Look for circles all around town.
The brightest circle shines at night.

Which Are Circles?

Circles are curved shapes that are perfectly round. Which of these signs are circles?

Welcome to Circle Town

OLLIE'S CLOCKS

Circle Sports

Circle Sports

SALE

Oscar's Bagels

Oscar's Bagels

28

Otto's Fruit

Go Nuts for Doughnuts!

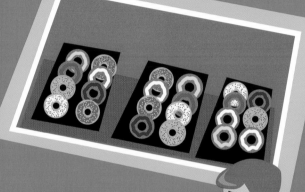

Circle Town is full of circles of all sizes. Where do you see circles?

PUBLIC WORKS

Glossary

ballpark (BAWL-park)—a place where baseball games are played

circle (SUR-kuhl)—a perfectly round shape

oval (OH-vuhl)—a curved shape that is not perfectly round

slash (SLASH)—a diagonal line over a picture to show that something is not allowed

stack (STAK)—to pile things up, one on top of another

traffic lights (TRAF-ik LITES)—red, yellow, and green lights that tell people and cars when to go and when to stop

Read More

Jones, Christianne C. *Around the Park: A Book about Circles.* Know Your Shapes. Minneapolis: Picture Window Books, 2006.

Kottke, Jan. *Circles.* City Shapes. New York: Welcome Books, 2000.

Salzmann, Mary Elizabeth. *Circles.* What Shape Is It? Edina, Minn.: Abdo, 2000.

Schuette, Sarah L. *Circles.* Shapes. Mankato, Minn.: Capstone Press, 2003.

Internet Sites

FactHound offers a safe, fun way to find Internet sites related to this book. All of the sites on FactHound have been researched by our staff.

Here's how:

1. Go to *www.facthound.com*
2. Select your grade level.
3. Type in this book ID **0736863680** for age-appropriate sites. You may also browse subjects by clicking on the letters, or by clicking on pictures and words.
4. Click on the **Fetch It** button.

FactHound will fetch the best sites for you!

Index